D0758436

CELEBRATING U.S. HOLIDAYS

Why Do We Celebrate LABOR DAY?

Frank Felice

PowerKiDS
press.

New York

Published in 2019 by The Rosen Publishing Group, Inc.
29 East 21st Street, New York, NY 10010

First Edition

Editor: Brianna Battista
Book Design: Reann Nye

Photo Credits: Cover Pacific Press/LightRocket/Getty Images; pp. 5, 21, 24 wavebreakmedia/Shutterstock.com; p. 6 Nestor Rizhniak/Shutterstock.com; p. 9 Courtesy of the Library of Congress; p. 10 Jetta Productions/Blend Images/Getty Images; p. 13 Dean Drobot/Shutterstock.com; pp. 14, 24 Ariel Skelley/DigitalVision/Getty Images; pp. 17, 23 Monkey Business Images/Shutterstock.com; pp. 18, 24 Kzenon/Shutterstock.com.

Cataloging-in-Publication Data

Names: Felice, Frank.
Title: Why do we celebrate Labor Day? / Frank Felice.
Description: New York : PowerKids Press, 2019. | Series: Celebrating U.S. holidays | Includes index.
Identifiers: LCCN ISBN 9781508166498 (pbk.) | ISBN 9781508166474 (library bound) | ISBN 9781538331811 (6 pack)
Subjects: LCSH: Labor day–United States–Juvenile literature.
Classification: LCC HD7791.F45 2019 | DDC 394.264–dc23

Manufactured in the United States of America

CPSIA Compliance Information: Batch #CS18PK: For Further Information contact Rosen Publishing, New York, New York at 1-800-237-9932

CONTENTS

Labor Day is the first Monday in September.

4

6

Labor Day celebrates the hard work of American people.

Labor Day also honors the fight for workers' rights.

9

American workers used to be in danger on the job. Today, we have rules to keep our workers safe.

Most people don't have to work on Labor Day.

13

Some cities have **parades**. The largest Labor Day parade in the country is in Pittsburgh.

Labor Day is also the start of football season.

Many people like to have **cookouts** on Labor Day.

Other people like to go to the **beach** on Labor Day.

How do you celebrate
Labor Day?

23

Words to Know

beach

cookout

parade

Index

Websites

Due to the changing nature of Internet links, PowerKids Press has developed an online list of websites related to the subject of this book. This site is updated regularly. Please use this link to access the list: www.powerkidslinks.com/ushol/labor